HATSUTAIKEN

HATSUTAIKEN

LEE BASSETT

Copper Canyon Press

Copyright © 1980 by Lee Bassett

ISBN 0-914742-51-5

for Kawabata Yasunari

"One feels the sadness at the end of glory"

FIELD

The world is junk. Everywhere we go, we stop and gather it. Right now we are on a field trip. As a matter of fact we are in a huge brown field, collecting junk. Crickets, seeds, cabbage butterflies. Look at us in this field. Niki, Big Bear, Little Bear, the collecting jars, the nets. We're so out of place here, we're the junk, and birds yell at us. We're scared of many many things and everything. Nansu pulls the guts from a milkweed pod and the bees come. Their cousins the wasps come. Then ants and spiders, a whole family that we don't belong in. We're lonely. A thousand eyes like the bee, a hundred hands like the spider, and still we're lonely. I tell you it's funny. The glands we are made of, the marrow and the veins and the flesh, are really all hands and eyes. And behind all of them is a lonely field where the empty heart moves, like music.

IN THE HOTEL

Not fair, not fair, the others are all on different floors, except Doc Bird. He's three doors down and quiet. They put me with Still-Smoking, who shoves the window up and yells. This is not home, but it is fun. Niki knocks and wants in, her TV doesn't work right, makes everyone look fat and old. This is our room. Still-Smoking won't let her sit on his bed, makes her park on the edge of a suitcase. You could see the top of the crack in her butt and parts of the bones that probably go all the way up to her head. She doesn't even know. Now the program is finished and Niki leaves. It's time to go to sleep. I go one last time to the window, to the loud city. I don't care where I am. In the hotel across the street an old man is also retiring. He carefully folds a dark blanket next to him in a double bed. It looks like the shape of a woman.

LETTER

Dear Kelly: How's the Mid-West? It's snowing like crazy here and school is a drag. Boy is math dumb. I've got a new boyfriend, well, I'm not sure if he likes me yet but he sure is cute! His name is Big Bear and he sits right in front of me in history. Yesterday, I was sitting in class just staring at his blond curls. Then he started breathing and I watched his back and shoulders go up and down. Then I started breathing right along with him, you know, the same way. God it made me feel weird inside! Oh yeah, I forgot to tell you, the other day me and Lizzy went into the gym after the boys finished practice. There was this strange smell in there, and I kind of liked it. God Kel, Lizzy liked it too. Well, tell me all about you and Bobby. Well, I gotta go but you better write soon! Can't wait for history class—Ha Ha!!
Love Ya, Niki.   P.S. He plays basketball!!

We must all line up, the tour-guide smiles. Because we could fall into the steak sauce, what a joke! Niki cups her hands over ears to stop the noise. Clink of glass jars, roar of the squeezer. Little Bear watches a lady cut cucumbers while she stares at us. More jokes about fingers and blood. Then the vinegar room, and Still-Smoking holds his nose. The guide points to a big vat of mustard that looks like paint. Big Bear reaches and pokes his finger in it and Doc Bird yells don't touch anything. Next, five different relishes, fragments of corn and peppers. Nansu feels sick. Then the pickle room; kosher, garlic, sweet chips, polish dills. Nansu looks ill, holds the lower part of her stomach. She feels something wet in her pants and looks down. A girlfriend notices and comes to help. Now you can get married, the friend laughs. Nansu turns red and says red. So many things are red, I never noticed, watermelons, sunsets, the bodies of new-born mice. Still-Smoking comes over and tells her about the ketchup on her pants. Doc Bird tells us not to touch anything.

You asked me to write about school and me and what I think about it. I don't want anyone to know me right now, so I'll just write about school. The bell rings and almost too much is happening. It's third period here, inside, but don't ask what time it is outside. All I want is to get through this crowd to my locker. There are a million kids and they drive me, they keep me twitching. Twitch twitch, here's Betty and Niki and Nansu. I'm hungry all the time. Sweaters everywhere and I'm sweating, just looking at them. I'd like to grab hold of something, I'd like to get out of this noise. Everyone is so cool. Here comes Eddie in his dumb wheelchair. He's got some disease forever, so we all have to get out of his way. We laugh because Eddie's such a spaz. There's Judy, taller than me and younger, I don't want her to know so I walk on my toes. Every one is so excited all the time and I'm just scared. I'm scared but no one knows. It's one thing to finally find your locker, it's another thing to try and remember the combination.

Monotony monotony, we are looking for the next thing to do. The food is gone, the softball game over and lost, and the sun starts home. Niki says the ants are bored. Doc Bird cleans the outside of a ketchup bottle. Niki says she doesn't understand; a strike is either swinging at a ball and missing it, or not swinging at it in the right place. Nansu combs her hair. Big Bear and Little Bear throw rocks at a cute chipmunk and then the lake. The girls walk far away from the crowd, sharing secrets and giggles. I love him, I want him, Niki says. Still-Smoking listens to his radio and the girls move over toward the sound. Music like the throbbing of the heart, Niki says. Then we pile in the car and start back to the city. Niki gets dropped off first and Doc Bird makes sure she gets into her apartment. We all stare up at the open window, waiting for a signal. Niki appears and takes her bathing suit off, the red dots on her chest open to the wind. She waves, not even looking at us.

CAMPING

Doc Bird takes us all camping, this time near Wild Bridge. We're on an island, clear water everywhere, we can hear Chatterbox Falls. Big Bear and Little Bear put tents up, wrong and then right, and Niki puts bread between her toes to feed the minnows. I'm with Still-Smoking, we are making a moss hut. We strip the green from the rocks and gather sticks. Nan-su is below us on the shore, tangled and fishing. Soon we finish the hut and sit quietly inside. Everything smells like earth and worms and heavy clothing. We are safe in here, camping is fun. Then Still-Smoking yells let's get Niki, and we wonder, should we. Soon she comes and joins us inside, inside our walls of moss. There is not much room for this new smell. All of a sudden as we sit there the sun goes down and Doc Bird calls. He sounds like he is drowning far away.

TARGET RANGE

Doc Bird passes around the bows and teaches us how to string them. Niki and Nansu fill red and blue targets with hay the color of sun. In this morning light both girls have hips, everything changes, yesterday they didn't seem to be there. The quivers are passed around, but we can't touch the arrows. Be careful, careful, Doc Bird shouts, they go exactly where you point them. Pretending to be Indian, Big Bear reaches behind himself in slow motion and lifts an arrow from his quiver. Slowly he turns and draws the string back. Everything is in one motion, first the faint new moustache appearing on his upper lip, then the outburst of hungry animal, then the long thin fire held tight in his hands. Little Bear looks scared. Then the girls finish stuffing the circles and start to walk back. Their arms are wet with hay. Doc Bird shows us how to shoot without the arrow, the right posture, the right motion. We all lift our bows and point. The girls are there and they look up. We point at the long fright in their eyes and let the string go.

DIARY

Oct 23. Lonely lonely, sick. Oct 24. I don't know why, but even when I'm with friends I'm alone. Oct 25. I'm so restless I'm afraid of doors. God, I still sleep with the light on! Talked with Jenny today, she told me about some phrase she found in a book; afternoons are too long. That says it all. Oct 28. Saw a movie in school today about the proper way to sit! God, I tried it at home in a mirror but it didn't feel right. I think I'm getting to distrust mirrors. Nov 2. Jenny wore really tight jeans today. Everyone stared. Wish I didn't have balloon hips. Nov 4. A weird weird day. Today I saw an old man crossing the street. He had a cane and strange looking shoes. Boy was he walking slow! When I passed him he tried to grab me, and that's why I said get away old man. I'm sorry I said it now, but boy I sure don't want to be like him. Nov 5. Went to the beach with the guys, really had fun. On the way back we sang every song that came on the radio.

FISHING

Doc Bird takes us fishing, really boring. We stop in a supersave for pop and worms, then drive forever. One dirt road after another and Nansu feeds the worms some pop. We find the lake and pile out. Poles and hooks everywhere. Doc Bird untangles the mess and we put worms on; Niki hates it and Big Bear has to help. Fishing is dumb. Soon the lines are in the water, bobbers waiting. They dance silent and Still-Smoking throws rocks at his own reflection and yawns. Not much is happening. First we think the worms are dead and then we think there aren't any fish. Who cares. Little Bear and Nansu leave their poles to go climb trees. Little Bear has never climbed before, and he is scared. He's clumsy and almost falls. His face is scared. Soon at the top with the limbs bending crazy, he's amazed at how stiff the thing between his legs is. His hands are shaking. The world shivers. Leaves twitch and seem to talk. Then he stays up there until we are ready to go, until he is calm. Monkey, we called him, please come down, monkey never caught a fish. Later he told some of us he'd like to climb trees again.

May 3. We beat Longfellow ten to two, we creamed them! Took Nansu to a strange movie, actually met her there. I don't know if I like her or not, I feel weird and excited. We held hands and stuff, and I sweated, boy did I pour! Sometimes I'd rather talk than touch, I get so scared, she must have noticed. Jesus, it was exciting, touching that smoothness of hers. Sometimes though, there's a real pain I have inside, just touching her. A strange panic, something really stupid and then something really clean about it, I don't know. It's sort of fun and sort of not. For no reason I was worn out, tired. I hope no one finds out. May 6. After practice I went over to Nansu's house. Her mom's car was gone. I was feeling good about us going together so I just walked right in the front door. Nansu was there alright, on this big couch with Big Bear. I was so scared I ran. I ran and cried and ran. My feet hurt. I stopped and called the telephone operator and asked her to just talk to me for a moment. She asked me if I liked baseball and if I had a favorite team and if so what was it.

FARM

All of us visit a farm, it's way out in the country; you know, lonely. We get there and run to the wood fence where the horses run. They stop and let us pet their red necks as they sweat. Doc Bird teaches us how to hold an apple for them. They slobber. Then we get to feed the pigs. Their eyes look smart or frightened or both. Still-Smoking rubs the back of one pig and smells his hand; smells like bacon. Then chickens in a dirty white house and boy it stinks. Big Bear gets to milk a cow. He pretends he's in a dance as he squeezes a teat and milk goes everywhere. Then we play in the hayloft. It's dark and has a dusty ghost smell. Niki and Nansu go behind a big stack of bales and the rest of us play tag and jump way down in the hay. It's hot in here but we climb up ladders and jump again. We go wild. We throw hay. Above us in a sweltering corner the girls are quiet. They know how hot it is. For a moment they open their shirts for a cool breeze. Breeze breeze, just for a second they look at the size of their breasts. The smell of the whole barn jumps from the bails. Below us where we can see the bus waiting, some cows bellow for more corn.

We are all here at the symphony, everyone's dressed up. Every time we move, Doc Bird says Shhhhh. We look back and see a thousand of us looking backwards. We giggle right here. Nansu is ten rows in front, sitting with Little Bear. Soon old men and women in black start tuning up and a white-haired man walks out. We clap. Then the music starts pouring over us, boom. The chairs feel larger, the room is not here. Nansu stares up at the carved ceiling and her hair falls behind her chair. Boom, it looks soft. Somehow the music and her hair are the same thing for a moment, and boom, we believe our eyes and ears. We know it's bad for us because everything we gather is junk. But today is beautiful and that's all. As if all we ever do is breathe music.

HATSUTAIKEN

Means first physical experience. Some of these prose poems have appeared in *Montana Review*, *Willow Springs*, and *Gilt Edge*. Issued in a signed edition of three hundred copies, this chapbook was designed and printed by Sam Hamill and Tree Swenson. The type is Italian Old Style, the paper is Rives white, and the presswork was completed under the sign of Taurus.

MCMLXXX